Francis Frith's
Woodbridge

CAROL and MICHAEL WEAVER are teachers of History and came to Woodbridge in 1969. They were involved with the setting up of a museum in Woodbridge, the restoration of Woodbridge Tide Mill and the founding of the Sutton Hoo Society. They have written a considerable number of local guides and monographs, including a history of The Seckford Foundation and of Ransomes of Ipswich, the celebrated engineering giants. Their illustrated lectures on Sutton Hoo have entertained, variously, audiences on cruise ships, Womens' Institutes throughout East Anglia and the students and staff of a prestigious American university. They do have interests outside local history, and these include Swansea City Football Club, Star Trek, their two daughters Robin and Bryony and Rosie, a celebrated cat.

Seager's Shop on Market Hill 1929 82963

Photographic Memories

Francis Frith's
Woodbridge

———————

Carol and Michael Weaver

First published in the United Kingdom in 2002 by
The Francis Frith Collection

Paperback Edition 2002
ISBN 1-85937-498-0

British Library Cataloguing in Publication Data

Francis Frith's Woodbridge
Carol and Michael Weaver

The Francis Frith Collection
Frith's Barn, Teffont,
Salisbury, Wiltshire SP3 5QP
Tel: +44 (0) 1722 716 376
Email: info@francisfrith.co.uk
www.francisfrith.com

Printed and bound in Great Britain

Front Cover: **Woodbridge, The Thoroughfare 1894** 33374

Contents

Francis Frith: *Victorian Pioneer*

FRANCIS FRITH, Victorian founder of the world-famous photographic archive, was a complex and multi-talented man. A devout Quaker and a highly successful Victorian businessman, he was both philosophic by nature and pioneering in outlook.

By 1855 Francis Frith had already established a wholesale grocery business in Liverpool, and sold it for the astonishing sum of £200,000, which is the equivalent today of over £15,000,000. Now a multi-millionaire, he was able to indulge his passion for travel. As a child he had pored over travel books written by early explorers, and his fancy and imagination had been stirred by family holidays to the sublime mountain regions of Wales and Scotland. 'What a land of spirit-stirring and enriching scenes and places!' he had written. He was to return to these scenes of grandeur in later years to 'recapture the thousands of vivid and tender memories', but with a different purpose. Now in his thirties, and captivated by the new science of photography, Frith set out on a series of pioneering journeys to the Nile regions that occupied him from 1856 until 1860.

Intrigue and Adventure

He took with him on his travels a specially-designed wicker carriage that acted as both dark-room and sleeping chamber. These far-flung journeys were packed with intrigue and adventure. In his life story, written when he was sixty-three, Frith tells of being held captive by bandits, and of fighting 'an awful midnight battle to the very point of surrender with a deadly pack of hungry, wild dogs'. Sporting flowing Arab costume, Frith arrived at Akaba by camel seventy years before Lawrence, where he encountered 'desert princes and rival sheikhs, blazing with jewel-hilted swords'.

During these extraordinary adventures he was assiduously exploring the desert regions bordering the Nile and patiently recording the antiquities and peoples with his camera. He was the first photographer to venture beyond the sixth cataract. Africa was still the mysterious 'Dark Continent', and Stanley and Livingstone's historic meeting was a decade into the future. The conditions for picture taking confound belief. He laboured for hours in his wicker dark-room in the sweltering heat of the desert, while the volatile chemicals fizzed dangerously in their trays. Often he was forced to work in remote tombs and caves where conditions were cooler. Back in London he exhibited his photographs and was 'rapturously cheered' by members of the Royal Society. His reputation as

a photographer was made overnight. An eminent modern historian has likened their impact on the population of the time to that on our own generation of the first photographs taken on the surface of the moon.

Venture of a Life-Time

Characteristically, Frith quickly spotted the opportunity to create a new business as a specialist publisher of photographs. He lived in an era of immense and sometimes violent change. For the poor in the early part of Victoria's reign work was a drudge and the hours long, and people had precious little free time to enjoy themselves. Most had no transport other than a cart or gig at their disposal, and had not travelled far beyond the boundaries of their own town or village. However,

by the 1870s, the railways had threaded their way across the country, and Bank Holidays and half-day Saturdays had been made obligatory by Act of Parliament. All of a sudden the ordinary working man and his family were able to enjoy days out and see a little more of the world.

With characteristic business acumen, Francis Frith foresaw that these new tourists would enjoy having souvenirs to commemorate their days out. In 1860 he married Mary Ann Rosling and set out with the intention of photographing every city, town and village in Britain. For the next thirty years he travelled the country by train and by pony and trap, producing fine photographs of seaside resorts and beauty spots that were keenly bought by millions of Victorians. These prints were painstakingly pasted into family albums and pored over during the dark nights of winter, rekindling precious memories of summer excursions.

The Rise of Frith & Co

Frith's studio was soon supplying retail shops all over the country. To meet the demand he gathered about him a small team of photographers, and published the work of independent artist-photographers of the calibre of Roger Fenton and Francis Bedford. In order to gain some understanding of the scale of Frith's business one only has to look at the catalogue issued by Frith & Co in 1886: it runs to some 670 pages, listing not only many thousands of views of the British Isles but also many photographs of most European countries, and China, Japan, the USA and Canada – note the sample page shown above from the hand-written *Frith & Co* ledgers detailing pictures taken. By 1890 Frith had created the greatest specialist photographic publishing company in the

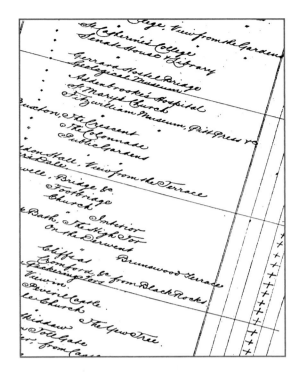

Frith's death, a new card measuring 5.5 x 3.5 inches became the standard format, but it was not until 1902 that the divided back came into being, with address and message on one face and a full-size illustration on the other. *Frith & Co* were in the vanguard of postcard development, and Frith's sons Eustace and Cyril continued their father's monumental task, expanding the number of views offered to the public and recording more and more places in Britain, as the coasts and countryside were opened up to mass travel.

Francis Frith died in 1898 at his villa in Cannes, his great project still growing. The archive he created continued in business for another seventy years. By 1970 it contained over a third of a million pictures of 7,000 cities, towns and villages. The massive photographic record Frith has left to us stands as a living monument to a special and very remarkable man.

world, with over 2,000 outlets — more than the combined number that Boots and W H Smith have today! The picture on the right shows the *Frith & Co* display board at Ingleton in the Yorkshire Dales. Beautifully constructed with mahogany frame and gilt inserts, it could display up to a dozen local scenes.

Postcard Bonanza

The ever-popular holiday postcard we know today took many years to develop. In 1870 the Post Office issued the first plain cards, with a pre-printed stamp on one face. In 1894 they allowed other publishers' cards to be sent through the mail with an attached adhesive halfpenny stamp. Demand grew rapidly, and in 1895 a new size of postcard was permitted called the court card, but there was little room for illustration. In 1899, a year after

Frith's Archive: *A Unique Legacy*

FRANCIS FRITH'S legacy to us today is of immense significance and value, for the magnificent archive of evocative photographs he created provides a unique record of change in 7,000 cities, towns and villages throughout Britain over a century and more. Frith and his fellow studio photographers revisited locations many times down the years to update their views, compiling for us an enthralling and colourful pageant of British life and character.

We tend to think of Frith's sepia views of Britain as nostalgic, for most of us use them to conjure up memories of places in our own lives with which we have family associations. It often makes us forget that to Francis Frith they were records of daily life as it was actually being lived in the cities, towns and villages of his day. The Victorian age was one of great and often bewildering change for ordinary people, and though the pictures evoke an impression of slower times, life was as busy and hectic as it is today.

We are fortunate that Frith was a photographer of the people, dedicated to recording the minutiae of everyday life. For it is this sheer wealth of visual data, the painstaking chronicle of changes in dress, transport, street layouts, buildings, housing, engineering and landscape that captivates us so much today. His remarkable images offer us a powerful link with the past and with the lives of our ancestors.

Today's Technology

Computers have now made it possible for Frith's many thousands of images to be accessed almost instantly. In the Frith archive today, each photograph is carefully 'digitised' then stored on a CD Rom. Frith archivists can locate a single photograph amongst thousands within seconds. Views can be catalogued and sorted under a variety of categories of place and content to the immediate benefit of researchers.

Inexpensive reference prints can be created for them at the touch of a mouse button, and a wide range of books and other printed materials assembled and published for a wider, more general readership - in the next twelve months over a hundred Frith local history titles will be published! The day-to-day workings of the archive are very different from how they were in Francis Frith's time: imagine the herculean task of sorting through eleven tons of glass negatives as Frith had to do to locate a particular sequence of pictures! Yet the

See Frith at www.francisfrith.com

archive still prides itself on maintaining the same high standards of excellence laid down by Francis Frith, including the painstaking cataloguing and indexing of every view.

It is curious to reflect on how the internet now allows researchers in America and elsewhere greater instant access to the archive than Frith himself ever enjoyed. Many thousands of individual views can be called up on screen within seconds on one of the Frith internet sites, enabling people living continents away to revisit the streets of their ancestral home town, or view places in Britain where they have enjoyed holidays. Many overseas researchers welcome the chance to view special theme selections, such as transport, sports, costume and ancient monuments.

We are certain that Francis Frith would have heartily approved of these modern developments in imaging techniques, for he himself was always working at the very limits of Victorian photographic technology.

The Value of the Archive Today

Because of the benefits brought by the computer, Frith's images are increasingly studied by social historians, by researchers into genealogy and ancestory, by architects, town planners, and by teachers and schoolchildren involved in local history projects.

In addition, the archive offers every one of us an opportunity to examine the places where we and our families have lived and worked down the years. Highly successful in Frith's own era, the archive is now, a century and more on, entering a new phase of popularity.

The Past in Tune with the Future

Historians consider the Francis Frith Collection to be of prime national importance. It is the only archive of its kind remaining in private ownership and has been valued at a million pounds. However, this figure is now rapidly increasing as digital technology enables more and more people around the world to enjoy its benefits.

Francis Frith's archive is now housed in an historic timber barn in the beautiful village of Teffont in Wiltshire. Its founder would not recognize the archive office as it is today. In place of the many thousands of dusty boxes containing glass plate negatives and an all-pervading odour of photographic chemicals, there are now ranks of computer screens. He would be amazed to watch his images travelling round the world at unimaginable speeds through network and internet lines.

The archive's future is both bright and exciting. Francis Frith, with his unshakeable belief in making photographs available to the greatest number of people, would undoubtedly approve of what is being done today with his lifetime's work. His photographs, depicting our shared past, are now bringing pleasure and enlightenment to millions around the world a century and more after his death.

Woodbridge and the River Deben
An Introduction

Up the river Deben, from the windswept shingle banks and tidal flats, the mariner searches his way by a winding channel, and the fields and woods close about him and replace the long sea-horizons. Landing at Woodbridge at high water he has approached by the same fairway as the adventurers and traders of the middle ages, ... an old-world fairway, that is now as then it was. This is a spot that is very England.

Alker Tripp: *Suffolk Sea-Borders*

THE sailing fraternity would agree today with the 1930s writer Alker Tripp that the only way to approach Woodbridge is up the River Deben. An unforgiving shingle bar at the mouth of the river and capricious tidal flows welcome the unwary and the experienced sailor alike. The reward for crossing the bar, however, is to sail up one of the most historic rivers in England, the landscapes on both sides remarkably unchanged over hundreds of years. Finally the church tower of St Mary's and the weather-boarded tide mill welcome the traveller to a town whose timber-framed and Georgian buildings and warm ambience never fail to please.

In the age of the railway train and motor car Woodbridge may have turned its face from the River Deben, but its history and character and its spirit are closely bound to that river. In the year 625 a great Saxon rowing vessel was dragged up the banks of the river opposite the present town, and in what was the last great pagan burial of our history, King Raedwald was laid to rest in that boat amid his glittering jewels and shining armour. Our area was the power-base of the Wuffings, whom he ruled, and it would not be fanciful to suggest that the newly-founded community opposite the royal burial ground bore the name of Woden's brygg, Woden's town, a tribute to their great and fierce god.

From the Middle Ages to the 17th century, ships

were built for the Royal Navy. A substantial flotilla sailed down the river in 1346 to fight for Edward III at the siege of Calais, and in 1588, when the Armada dared to pass by, Woodbridge ships are said to have sailed out to lend their weight to the harassment of the Spaniards. A Woodbridge sailor, John Foxe, born at the Crown Inn, endured 14 years of imprisonment at the hands of the Turks before engineering a most famous escape, rescuing 300 fellow Christians and returning to England a hero of the day, to be well rewarded by Elizabeth I. Later, Samuel Pepys sent his agent, Peter Pett, to supervise the construction of ships for Charles II, and a Woodbridge ship helped to capture Gibraltar in 1704. A small number of daring pirates and a considerable number of smugglers are associated with the river's history.

The influence of one Tudor citizen looms large in the story of Woodbridge. Thomas Seckford, born in 1516, served Queen Elizabeth I as Master of the Court of Requests. He amassed a great fortune in a successful legal career, and just before his death he obtained letters patent for the foundation of an almshouse in Woodbridge, where thirteen poor men would be cared for. He endowed the foundation with his property in Clerkenwell, Middlesex, yielding an annual income of over £100. No one could have known that London would engulf Clerkenwell in the years ahead and the rental values increase quite dramatically. For exactly a century, family members struggled to regain their lost inheritance, and the citizens of the town showed equal determination to keep it - and succeeded. In the 19th century, rents from the Clerkenwell estate, which had undergone considerable 'improvement', furnished the town with two elegant almshouses and a number of other amenities, including a dispensary for the sick, a library and even a town pump on the Market Hill. In 1864 there were further funds to boost the ailing finances of the Free School Charity, and a new school was constructed on the Burkitt Road.

After the excitements of the Napoleonic Wars which ended in 1815, and which had seen the construction of huge barracks in the town, Woodbridge slipped back to comfortable somnolence. At a grand auction sale, the detritus of a generation of war was sold off: discerning observers may still find the odd barrack building serving as a garden shed or outhouse in certain town gardens.

Edward FitzGerald was one notable resident of the town in the quiet Victorian period. He translated the verses of Omar Khayyam, a Persian poet-philosopher of the 12th century. The poem, privately printed and distributed, languished unsold for some years, but when it was 'discovered' it became the intellectual craze of its time. The Poet Laureate, Alfred Lord Tennyson, visited FitzGerald in Woodbridge, staying at the Bull Hotel. The proprietor, John Grout, gave him a conducted tour of the inn and stables. He later asked 'old Fitz' who this famous guest was and was told haughtily that it was the Poet Laureate. 'Well, he didn't fare to know much about hosses,' was the laconic reply. FitzGerald endured the lack of a cultural and intellectual atmosphere in the town, but gathered a small circle of like-minded literary friends about him - the Woodbridge wits - who included Bernard Barton, the Quaker poet. The townspeople held him in some awe and tolerated his rather eccentric behaviour. He understood Woodbridge folk well, and named his small sailing boat 'Scandal' after the chief preoccupation of Woodbridgians!

The royal jubilees of 1887 and 1897 brought the town together in a massive show of enthusiasm and celebration. Open-air feasts and grand parades were the order of the day. A local cobbler, T D Symonds, recorded these events and others in doggerel verse which he published in booklet form or in the local newspaper. He is a poet still awaiting a wider audience! Woodbridge seemed rich in 'characters' during the last years of the century. A young teacher at the Woodbridge Grammar School, William Balgarnie, became the model for the greatest fictional teacher of them all - Mr Chips.

When William Dutt, the late-Victorian traveller and writer, visited Woodbridge he described it as 'a delightful little town, one of the prettiest little country towns in England. Nestling on the slopes of what in Suffolk must be called a hilly district, the sun always seems to shine on it'. Lulled by the quiet pace of life in Woodbridge which he observed, Dutt was forced to conclude that Woodbridge had 'not played any active part in the stirring events of East Anglian history.' Here he was mistaken. Certainly, many Woodbridgians had been at the centre of national events. Of course, many 'stirring events' lay ahead too. In 1915 the town was bombed by a German Zeppelin. Six citizens were killed. There are not many earlier examples of this new type of warfare where civilians are targeted in an aerial attack. Two soldiers returning home on leave from the Western Front found that their mother had been killed in the raid - cruel irony indeed.

Later in the century, the town would be surrounded by airfields. In the 1930s the local schoolboys would cycle to Martlesham to catch a glimpse of the experimental aircraft taking off. Douglas Bader and Peter Townsend were just two of the great pilots who flew out of Martlesham. At Bawdsey Manor, at the mouth of the Deben, vital experiments and testing of radar changed the course of history. Americans remained at the Woodbridge and Bentwaters airbases until 1993, and the gaping economic void left by their departure has still not been satisfactorily filled.

Woodbridge adjusted slowly to the demands of the 20th century. The town grew steadily and enjoyed the advantage of a magnificent 'by-pass road' in the 1930s. In the late 1920s there were still barges to be found unloading cargoes at the Tide Mill Quay. The ancient mill itself, now the last of its type, worked until 1957, and stands as a symbol of how small towns like Woodbridge sought new commercial avenues as old industries collapsed. The tide mill opened in 1972, after an extensive restoration programme completed without even a hint of a lottery grant, as a tourist attraction. Fifteen thousand visitors annually admire the technology of an earlier age.

Woodbridge and the villages of the River Deben have seen industries flourish, fade and then die. The coprolite trade, cement-making, rope-making, ship-building; the list is endless. At the end of the 20th century, leisure and tourism emerged as the Deben's greatest asset. Certainly the spirit of invention which created radar in our area is now to be found at Adastral Park, Martlesham where the BT tower is a familiar landmark. The proximity to Ipswich and London beyond has attracted a new wave of commuters. Each year however, greater efforts are made to bring in visitors. In Woodbridge, an excellent small town museum and the Suffolk Horse Museum, both on the Market Hill, the Tide Mill on the Deben and Buttrum's Windmill act as hosts to the discerning tourist. The opening of a magnificent visitor centre at Sutton Hoo in 2002 is set to help revive the fortunes of the Suffolk Sandlings. There were 7000 visitors in the first week!

The advent of out-of-town supermarkets inevitably changed the face of 'retail' Woodbridge and Wickham Market. As late as the 1960s, a Woodbridge resident could find all his essential needs on the Market Hill: groceries, newspapers, medicines, even fish and chips. Taylor's of Wickham Market was a famous institution, serving the small town and the villages about. Antique shops, art galleries and the offices of estate agents now stand where once retail dynasties flourished.

Turn your steps towards the river, however, and the spirit of earlier times can quickly be discovered. Examine the pace of river life from the comfort of the Maybush at Waldringfield; walk the Smugglers Run at Martlesham Creek, or the riverside path from Kyson to Woodbridge. Better still, follow Alker Tripp's journey in a small boat from Bawdsey to Woodbridge up that river that is remarkably unchanged over centuries. Then you might agree with him that, even in the twenty-first century, this is still 'a spot that is very England.'

From the Tower of St Mary's Church 1894 33985
The chimneys of the Abbey point skywards on the lower right, and the line of Church Street can be easily traced. Woodbridge Tide Mill and its granary are clearly identifiable on the river, and beyond we can see the open spaces of the Suffolk Sandlings, including Sutton Hoo.

From the Sutton Shore 1894 33981
The tower of St Mary's and the spire of
St John's dominate the skyline of this
panoramic view. Commercial buildings and
private residences crowd the river's edge.
The weather-boarded tide mill stands
impressively in the foreground, looking
down the Deben.

The Deben Estuary

The ever-shifting bar at the mouth of the river has acted as a deterrent to all but the most determined explorer and eager maritime entrepreneur. It is strange to think that a great 90ft-long Anglo-Saxon rowing vessel, chosen for a royal burial, crossed the bar in 625AD and made its way up a river which man had yet to begin to claim as his own. Marshy inlets stranded Bawdsey, and smaller rivulets ran in to discover Trimley, Kirton and Bucklesham. The port of Goseford, first named by the Saxons and famous for its shipbuilding well into the Middle Ages, has disappeared under the watery creeks and reclaimed land.

The ingenious riverside dwellers of the Deben's history have harvested what they could from the shore and the valley slopes. Clay lumps called copperas were gathered for use in the dyeing industry. Coprolites, which are fossilised animal remains, were harvested by the thousands of tons and sent down the river and all over Britain as a valuable artificial fertiliser. At Waldringfield, a dozen kilns were once at work making cement. Up to 400 tons a day could be shipped out; a remarkable enterprise.

Today the estuary is alive with smaller leisure craft enjoying the freedom of the river or escaping to the sea.

Bawdsey, The Manor 1899 43242
The Victorian financier Cuthbert Quilter built this magnificent manor house which stands guard at the mouth of the River Deben. In the 20th century it was attacked both by the sea and by punitive death duties, and it was finally sold to the government in 1936. It was here that research into radar was carried out. Today it is an international school.

Waldringfield, The River Deben c1955 W438004
Modern man has not succeeded in intruding greatly or permanently upon the banks of the river. In the late 19th century the local river mud, mixed with chalk, made a fine cement. The chalk was often unloaded on the open beach. The industry collapsed about 1908, and Waldringfield returned to peace and quiet.

Waldringfield, The Sailing Club c1955 W438019
The club house is set up for racing at Deben Week. The keen spectators and the announcer's loudspeaker may be clearly seen. The weather-boarded building was replaced in 1981. The extravagantly coiffured figurehead we can just see on the gable now temporarily resides in the clubhouse, awaiting a permanent resting place.

Waldringfield, The River c1955 W438017
We are looking down river from the Sailing Club, where the competitors' boats are readied for a busy days' racing. The tide is rising, soon the river will be alive with the bobbing craft, as competition gets under way.

◄ **Waldringfield
Sandy Lane c1960**
W438038
The hedge may have
grown in 40 years, but
the old post office can
still be found in Sandy
Lane, although it has
very limited opening
hours these days. We
can only surmise how
important the post
office and general
stores were for most of
the 20th century, both
commercially and as a
vital centre for village
gossip.

◄ Waldringfield
The Maybush Inn c1955
W438011

This 15th-century pub serves the locals of Waldringfield and the many visitors who use the river; its location tells that here was the junction for one of the many ferries that crossed the Deben in earlier times. The Maybush has always been a very welcome landmark for sailors at the half-way point between Woodbridge and the mouth of the River Deben.

▼ Martlesham, The Creek
c1955 M267003

The shapely oak tree is gone, sad to say. The creek was a favoured haunt of smugglers in its time, and many a cask of brandy and 'Geneva' have been unloaded here and taken across to Ipswich. Today a walk for visitors along the path in the foreground is called 'the Smugglers Run', affording fine views towards Woodbridge.

◄ Martlesham
The Red Lion 1896
37325

The fierce red lion figurehead has looked down on generations of passing travellers and the wiser travellers who stopped. Local custom says that it was a prize from a Dutch ship wrecked at the Battle of Sole Bay in 1672. Some argue that it came from an Armada vessel; certainly, the heart of the building is late-Tudor.

Martlesham, The Hill c1955 M267007
It is sixty years after photograph No 37325, and the Red Lion Inn still stands guard at the junction. Sunsets are traditionally described by locals as being 'as red as the Martlesham Lion'. The road leading to Ipswich is remarkably unchanged to this day.

Martlesham, The Street c1955 M267001
Serenely quiet in 1955, this stretch of road became infamous in the 1970s and 1980s as the most congested road in the county, with traffic passing at a snail's pace for many hours a day. It serviced the American airbases at Woodbridge and Bentwaters, and was the main highway between Lowestoft and Ipswich. The village now has a by-pass.

Riverside Woodbridge

One local historian has said that 'you can never get away from the lingering saltiness which has seeped through the whole of the town's history.' Woodbridge has enjoyed a long tradition of ship-building. Ships of up to 200 tons burden were constructed here, and small repair yards may still be found. Peter Pett came to Woodbridge to supervise the construction of vessels for Charles II's navy. He put up at the Crown and married the proprietor's daughter! This riverside was also, for centuries, the door to the outside world; pilgrims sailed to young America, fishermen to Iceland, traders to the ports of northern Europe. Smugglers loved the convenience of Martlesham Creek and Kyson Point. Cargo vessels brought coals from Newcastle and carried away carrots and corn for the London market.

After the advent of the railway line in the 1850s and road transport in the early 20th century, the sight of laden barges on the river gradually became a memory only. The river bank played a vital role in the social life of the town, however; it was a meeting place for romantic young things, a parade for leaders of local fashion, a play and swimming area for the energetic. Today the members of thriving sailing clubs and keen joggers and the occasional mad, illegal cyclist occupy those same riverside paths.

Kyson 1908 60683
About a mile south of the town centre is Kyson Hill, an area of parkland and part of the old royal manor of Kingston given to the National Trust in 1934 by Mr R C Notcutt. The path is a favoured Sunday walk for Woodbridgians all the year round. Try it at dusk on a summer's evening.

▼ **The River Deben 1938** 88711
Racing during the annual regatta week in August; flags fly over the Deben
Yacht Club. The regatta is the highlight of the sailing season, and it has
been for nearly 200 years. It started as an entertainment for barge crews
and local water men, but it was opened up to all river users in the 1930s.

▼ **The Riverside Gardens and the Model Yacht Pond 1938** 88710
A popular leisure area for old and young alike. The model yacht pond and
neatly trimmed lawns and gardens made a safe play area for children and
a meeting place for their mums. Changing times and social priorities have
resulted in the loss of the order and neatness we see here.

▲ **The River Wall 1898**
42770
Here we see an unusually
empty riverside walk and
river. The band-stand
looks out over the river
and also the riverside
gardens. On selected
summer days before the
last war, the whole town
would turn out to sit and
enjoy the music from one
of the local bands.

◀ **The Boat Station 1894**
33372
A small vessel, the 'Hope', takes on cargo at one of the small wooden jetties along the river bank. A more substantial barge may be seen unloading at the tide mill. Oblivious to the activity around him, one gentleman prepares for a day's sailing on a rising tide.

The Avenue 1894 33380
This delightful tree-lined avenue, sometimes called Rope Walk, leads down to the riverside gardens and yacht pond and to the river beyond.

The Promenade 1925 78746

Ladies of leisure have tired of the river views, it seems. The Daily Sketch is of greater interest. Behind the band-stand is Everson's boatyard, one of the River Deben's institutions. One constant in every photograph of the river and river wall - is that the tide is always in. Today, swans would gently harass the readers in search of tit-bits.

The Beach and First Shelter 1898 42773

This is a play area for youngsters at full tide only. At low tide it is a sea of congealing mud. This photograph needs careful exploring. A gentleman prepares to take to the open river; young rascals fish for crabs; the shelter is sedately filled; there are paddlers and sunbathers and even a bored dog. The River Deben stretches away to the horizon.

The Beach and First Shelter 1898 42772
It must be Sunday; ladies, nannies and children are dressed to perfection. The cameraman has attracted a crowd of curious onlookers. 'Smile, everyone ... and keep still.' Look across the river to the Sutton shore, for undoubtedly some intrepid walkers have paid the ferryman to row them across on this day.

◄ **The Bathing Place 1894**
33986
This is, of course, on the Sutton side, opposite Woodbridge and beneath the Sutton Hoo royal cemetery. The beach itself is a graveyard - for old Woodbridge ships which have crossed the bar for the last time. Young swimmers loved the beach, and local marksmen also came over here to practice shooting into the safety of the soft, sandy cliffs.

◄ **From the Sutton Shore 1896** 37316
Those who do venture over the river have an unparalleled view of the town. This was a favoured spot for photographers and artists alike; a convenient spot too - just a few yards from the ferry, through the gap in the hedge on the left. No one wanted to be stranded by the falling tide.

▲ **A General View from the Sutton Shore 1894** 33983
Here we can admire the town from the quiet of the Sutton bank. The gas works, now dismantled, is visible in the centre. Facing us is the tide mill pond of seven and a half acres. Twice a day this pond filled, and the water was released at low tide to drive the great wooden wheel of the mill. This gave about eight hours milling a day. When the mill broke down in 1957 and proved too expensive to repair, the pond was sold off for use as a yacht marina.

The Ferry Dock and the River Deben 1965 W128080
The first shelter, without its elegant Victorian gabled roof, is seen on the right. The ferry dock tells of the new industry that sustains the riverside economy. Small leisure craft are repaired and titivated and moored here.

The Ferry Dock and the River Deben 1965 W128086
It does not take a lot of imagination to discern the skilful art of gentrifying small craft, adding cabins and living space. On the far side of the dock a crane prepares to lower a repaired vessel into the water. The mansard roof of the tide mill is just visible on the left-hand side.

Exploring Woodbridge

Woodbridge was a small but thriving settlement at the time of the Doomsday Book in 1087, and it grew steadily throughout the Middle Ages. The Black Canons of the Augustinian priory were an important feature of town life until the Dissolution of the Monasteries. Woodbridge enjoyed the benefits of a weekly market, and the annual St Audrey's Fair attracted visitors from far and wide. Cheap jewellery and St Audrey's lace were sold at this fair, items of such low quality that the word 'tawdry' came into being.

Timber-framed structures gave way to Georgian elegance in the 18th century. For many residents this meant no more than attaching a brick front to the old building. These false fronts can be readily identified around the town. The lover of old buildings will enjoy exploring Woodbridge, as it is a veritable catalogue of changing architectural styles and fashions.

After the quiet of the 19th century, the coming of the motor car was a shock to the town. The first car to visit, on an Easter tour with RAC members, broke down and was unceremoniously dragged into the Bull Hotel yard, the very yard which had supplied horses to the King of Italy. The locals were delighted; Woodbridge was the town of the horse, but all that had to change.

Cumberland Street 1925 78751
This fine residential area has many elegant Georgian houses, some of which were developed by officers stationed in Woodbridge at the time of the Napoleonic Wars. The fire station on the right was involved in a dramatic fire in 1922 when the 'C' Flight hangar at Martlesham Airfield caught fire. The Woodbridge Fire Brigade arrived with a horse-drawn engine and cab, the chief giving his orders by calls on a bugle.

▼ **Cumberland Street c1960** W128052
This is the commercial end of the street. The line of low-lying shops on the right
replaced Alfred Barnes Emporium, a huge Georgian structure destroyed by
fire in 1905. Garnhams Garage (left) and the site of the old post office on the
corner have also been demolished to house a bank and a Chinese restaurant.

▼ **Cumberland Street c1965** W128076
Just a little further in time and distance from No W128052 we have a closer view
of the Post Office, which boasts a 16th-century ceiling and staircase. It is now a
sorting office. The elegant Cumberland House beyond clearly reveals the efforts of
the fashion-conscious; an ornate Georgian facade has been added to the earlier
17th-century building. Opposite, Gordon House and Marston House are fine
examples of town houses of the Georgian period. F Masters, Monumental Mason
(centre right), produced headstones and funerary monuments until recently.

▲ **The Thoroughfare
1906** 53498
For centuries this has
been the commercial
heart and the main route
through Woodbridge.
This view from the Cross
Corner gives a glimpse
of the age and diversity
of the buildings and
the range of services.
The Crown Inn was an
imposing posting house,
the first stage beyond
Ipswich along the bustling
coaching route to Great
Yarmouth, a thirteen-hour
journey in 1812.

◀ **Cross Corner 1955**

W128021

Cross Corner is the junction of the Thoroughfare, Cumberland Street, Church Street and Quay Street. The lovely timber-framed 17th-century Cross Inn stands on the corner opposite the Crown. The uniformed traffic conductor is one of a small fraternity of renowned individuals who assumed this role following the birth of the motor car at the turn of the last century.

The Crown Hotel c1955 W128017
We can see the traffic conductor again helping pedestrians outside the Crown Hotel. Early in the 19th century the Prince Regent, later George IV, was a regular customer at the Crown; he was passing through on his way to the Marquis of Hertford's estate at Sudbourne, where the attractions were the estate's hunting facilities and the delightful Lady Hertford.

The Thoroughfare 1906 53499

In the quieter days of horse-drawn traffic, the Thoroughfare was a flourishing commercial centre with a huge range of small shops and businesses and domestic dwellings in combination. Notable (and just visible in the centre distance) are Loder's Printers, an establishment responsible for varied and significant records of Woodbridge's past, and the Royal Oak Inn, which traded until the 1930s. It became a wine bar in the 1980s under the proprietorship of the celebrated character actor Douglas Wilmer, and was appropriately named Sherlocks after his most famous role. Also prominent is the ornate rococo style of Lloyds Bank, an impressive late 19th century structure with its railings intact.

The Thoroughfare 1894 33374
Continuing eastwards along the Thoroughfare, we see a view showing pedestrians in Victorian working clothes and a procession of horses and carts. The shop fronts are distinctively late-Victorian, with Savill's boasting a beautiful and distinctive bow window. Adjacent to the furthest cart is an impressively ornate Victorian structure, then a china shop owned by the Morleys, an eminent Quaker family. Frank Morley became an distinguished mathematician and chess player and his son Christopher wrote a fascinating novel, 'Thoroughfare', in which he describes life in the china shop. The building is now owned by Barretts, and sells high quality furniture and furnishings.

▼ The Thoroughfare c1955 W128002

We are looking westwards towards Cross Corner from the middle section of the Thoroughfare. The shop fronts are largely unaltered. The large 18th-century gabled building at the top right-hand of the street is now F W Woolworth's.

▼ The Thoroughfare c1965 W128074

This view clearly shows Woolworth's and the International Stores, both establishments reflecting the addition of the larger all-purpose stores to small specialist shops. The Lloyds Bank building has a large and distinctive sign. The car park sign is indicative of the growth of the motor car and the need for parking space within the town centre.

▲ Church Street 1906
53497

Church Street, originally called Stone Street, winds gently up to the Market Hill from Cross Corner, a mixture of fine town houses and commercial buildings dating from the 16th century. The enormous building on the right has an early 17th-century core and an early 19th-century facade. It is now a branch of Barclays Bank.

◀ **Church Street 1906** 53500
A little further on we see
Saville's Ironmongery,
'The Handiest Shop in
Woodbridge.' At a later
date the old roof line was
restored and the bold
slogan lost. The columns
remain. The building is now
a travel agency. Further
along is Arnott House, a
3-storied, late 18th-century
dwelling, a fine example of
the quality of the domestic
architecture in the town.

Church Street c1960 W128051

Traffic lights and traffic signals and a few vehicles again illustrate the arrival of the motor car. Barclays Bank now
has a large sign, as does the Deben Tea Rooms, no longer operating, sad to say; but the 17th-century building now
houses a popular video rental shop, a sure sign of modernisation!

St Mary's Church and the Jubilee Monument 1894 33987

This impressive church in the Perpendicular style is a landmark in the centre of the town. Externally, the black flint flushwork of the huge 108ft tower and the north porch are notable. In the graveyard we will find the box tombs of the Clarkson family, pioneers of the anti-slavery movement in the 19th century. In the foreground, Queen Victoria stands in a secluded garden, looking imperiously towards the Bull Hotel.

St Mary's Church
The Interior 1896 37175

Since 1896, the rood screen has been moved and an elaborate font-cover installed. The once colourful font was severely damaged by the iconoclast William Dowsing in 1644, but it is still one of the finest examples in Suffolk.
The marble memorial in the south aisle commemorates Jeffrey Pitman, his two wives and his sons, and was made by the same family who constructed Shakespeare's memorial in Stratford.
A small and simple table-tomb may be found in the chancel - a rather inadequate memorial to the town's great benefactor, Thomas Seckford, who died in 1587.
The true monuments to his generosity are the Seckford buildings, which are well represented in this volume.

◄ **The Bull Hotel 1938**
88709
Many inns have stood on the Market Hill, but the Bull Hotel has been there for ever. This is where Tennyson stayed when he visited FitzGerald in the 19th century. The Sutton Hoo archaeologists in 1939 were guests here, and at least one drank a pint at the bar having in his pocket the gold belt buckle, one of England's most important treasures and discovered that very day.

Market Hill c1955 W128058
We have just left Church Street, and now face a vista of architectural diversity on the crowded Market Hill, to say nothing of unrestrained small-town commercial activity where the chemist and the pet-food purveyor, the paint and hardware store and the heating engineers all jockey for position. The parked cars on our right are those of the customers of the Bull Hotel.

The Bull Hotel on Market Hill c1955 W128018
A cyclist is caught in time, struggling up the hill. Behind the Bull Hotel, to the left, glance down New Street where the steel-yard is just visible. The ivy-clad Old Court House stands on the corner; now it is sheltered accommodation for the elderly. Mr Pearce the chemist has moved on.

The Shire Hall 1925 78749
A Great War trophy points dangerously at us and at the Bull Hotel behind us. Look for the two cell doors on either side of the grand entrance to the Shire Hall. Saturday night rowdies could expect to cool down there. Useful shops abound. The King's Head Inn at the top of the hill (left) is a 15th-century structure and has many stories to tell.

The Shire Hall 1938
88707
Mr Pearce the chemist has taken over from W R Weatherley. Nettleinghams and Seagers next door survived for another fifty years. The quiet open square has today succumbed to traffic islands and signs pointing in all directions. The Shire Hall houses Woodbridge Town Council on the ground floor, and on the first floor where the magistrates once passed sentence is the Suffolk Horse Museum.

The Shire Hall 1908
60685
The Shire Hall dominates Market Hill. It is a late Tudor structure, much changed. The curved steps just about hide evidence of the open arcades that were part of the original building. In more recent times, the Magistrates held court on the first floor. 'Going up the steps' had a sinister meaning for local malefactors.

◀ **The Shire Hall c1965**
W128094
Thomas Seckford's coat of arms above the first floor entrance reminds us that it was Seckford who moved the courts from Melton to the heart of Woodbridge, and buil[t] this hall to house them above an arcaded open corn market. Markets have been held on this spot for hundreds of years; market day is Thursday.

▼ **The Market Hill c1955**
W128035
The impressive 'Tudor' timbering in the central building was constructed in the 1930s above 18th-century shop fronts; the whole facade covers a 16th-century structure. Only in Woodbridge could this happen! The gable end of th[e] Angel Inn, visible at the top o[f] Angel Lane where a smart ca[r] is almost suicidally parked, is assuredly original, however.

Buttrums Mill c1955
W128042
Standing guard on the
northern outskirts of the
town, this impressive
brick tower mill which
dates from 1816 is a
popular visitor attraction.
The sails still turn,
though the mill-stones
have been disengaged
inside. The cap turns
to the wind, so that
every day admirers of
the mill see the sails
at a different angle.
Buttrums Mill worked
commercially as late as
1928.

The Old Pump 1965 W128055
When the Seckford Charity received vastly increased revenues from its London
estates in the 19th century, this pump was erected for the townspeople at a cost of
£250. At the base you will see a drinking trough for 'horses, dogs and cattle passing
through the town'. Cars, scooters and bicycles have brought shoppers onto the hill
where everyone's daily needs could be met.

The Bell Inn 1894
33375

The Bell Inn stands on New Street, a road first mentioned in the Court Rolls of 1549 and built to allow easier access from the River Deben to Market Hill. The timber-framed building probably dates from the same time. Tradition speaks of an earlier name, the Three Goats Inn, before 1830. The date of the distinctive timber-framed steelyard is uncertain, but most examples can be traced to the early 17th century. We can see that the sling chains used to raise the full wagons are still evident, though it was last in use in the 1880s. The white timber-framed building beyond the inn is the Bridewell. It was used as a poorhouse in the mid 17th century, and served as a temporary jail for the Dutch prisoners after the Battle of Sole Bay.

The Steelyard 1908 60686
This view of the Bell Inn and its distinctive steelyard looks up New Street towards the Market Hill. The cobbled fronts which abutted the buildings have disappeared since the Frith visit of 1894. By the time of this photograph, only the elderly residents could remember seeing wagons of corn being weighed fully laden, and then again after emptying their contents at the corn market on Market Hill.

New Street 1925 78750

This view looks down New Street as the road dips sharply towards the Thoroughfare. On the left is a line of small specialist shops and a working garage. The garage in the building on the right-hand side belongs to the Bull Hotel. Formerly the stables, it also houses the grave of an 18th-century ostler, George Carlow, a Sabbatarian who chose not to be buried on consecrated ground.

**The Old Bell and Steelyard
New Street 1929** 82959

In 1925 the Bell Inn and its steelyard were united in name, and the public house has been known as the Old Bell and Steelyard since that time. It is the most photographed public house in Woodbridge, both for its attractive timbering and its jettied or overhanging first floor and also, of course, for its distinctive adjoining steelyard. This steelyard is estimated to have had a loading capacity of 3 tons. A similar steelyard in Soham is said to have raised an elephant in the 1880s. The inn's outward appearance has changed very little over the years.

The Wesleyan Chapel 1896 37322

Woodbridge boasts a fine collection of nonconformist chapels, none finer than that of the Methodist denomination, built in 1871. The railings have now gone - victims of the need for metal during the last war. We will find streets named after the prime ministers Gladstone and Disraeli behind the chapel, and there is evidence of light industry on the right in Sun Lane.

St John's Church 1925 78757
The religious life of Woodbridge is said to have undergone a revitalisation in the 1830s, and St John's Church was constructed to reflect this. The church clock was stopped by the Zeppelin raid of 1915, a reminder to all locals of the exact moment of the attack. The spire, rising to 138ft, was declared unsafe thirty years ago and demolished.

St John's Church, the Interior 1896 37176
Not long after the photographer left, the galleries which we see on the left and right were removed. From this church's consecration in 1846, its services have always reflected the more evangelical wing of the Church of England.

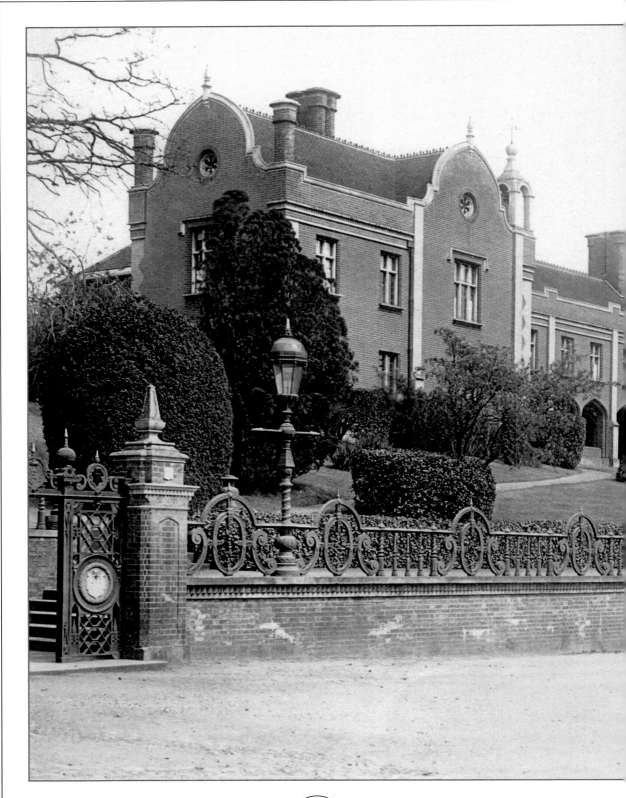

The Distinguished Residents of Woodbridge

The Seckford Connection and Edward FitzGerald

It is strange to think that the two of the greatest poems in the English language have strong links with the Woodbridge area. The Anglo-Saxon poem 'Beowulf', with its vivid descriptions of great royal burials in boats and barrows, has huge echoes in the Sutton Hoo ship burial site opposite Woodbridge. The great Victorian masterpiece 'The Rubaiyat of Omar Khayyam' was written by Woodbridge resident Edward FitzGerald – it is a brilliant free translation of a Persian original. These poems are enjoyed to this day.

The Seckford Hospital 1894 33378
This early Victorian almshouse with its magnificent iron railings is the largest building in Woodbridge. It was constructed with the vast funds accruing from Clerkenwell in London, the site of Thomas Seckford's original estate endowed to the charity in 1587. Its construction marked the first stage in a series of massive benefits which Woodbridge would enjoy in the 19th century as a result of Seckford's generosity.

FitzGerald was born at nearby Bredfield, and lived there and at Boulge before moving to the Market Hill and eventually to a house on the outskirts of the town, Little Grange. He secretly enjoyed the fame which his poem justly brought and relished the company of fellow poets and intellectuals, many of whom visited him in Woodbridge. His letters tell of the frustrations of life in Woodbridge, but he put up with its short-comings because from his experience, life in London was even worse. The Frith photographer made a complete Edward FitzGerald pilgrimage in 1929, recording every building associated with the great man. It is a most valuable pictorial record.

Centuries before, Thomas Seckford, a leading courtier and legal figure in the court of Queen Elizabeth, built an impressive town house in Woodbridge, and his generosity moulded the future of the town. Woodbridge School in particular was rescued in the 1860s with an injection of Seckford funds. Robert Beale of Woodbridge also served Queen Elizabeth; he carried the death warrant of Mary Queen of Scots to Fotheringaye, where he was the official royal witness to the most famous execution of the century.

In recent years at least one former Director General of the BBC and a famous newsreader and personality have enjoyed retirement in the town. Media celebrities live here today, but it would be impudent to drop names or invade their privacy.

The Abbey 1896 37177
This was Thomas Seckford's town house, built on the site of the mediaeval abbey, and dated 1564. The house has enjoyed a long and interesting history, boasts at least one ghost, and now serves as the junior department of Woodbridge School, where 300 pupils attend. Many Victorian additions can be spotted on the building, including the ornate brick finials on the roof.

Seckford Hall 1896 37320

The impressive seat of the Seckford family lies just outside the town. A gentleman's residence for most of its life, some old pictures show it in a very run-down state, little more than a grand farm-house. After the Second World War and military occupation it was revitalised in the care of the Bunn family, who have created a magnificent hotel and leisure complex while retaining the historical ambience of this wonderful building.

Woodbridge School, Marryott House c1960 W128043

Robert Marryott founded the Free School, Woodbridge, in 1662. When the school moved to a new site outside town in 1864, the building was named after him. One hundred pupils attended on the first day; today there are more than one hundred teachers. In 1974 Woodbridge School admitted girls. The school boasts a fine academic record, and is renowned widely for its sporting and musical accomplishments.

▼ Woodbridge School, School House 1896 37178

School House was the wonder of its age when it opened as the headmaster's house and boarding house in January 1895. It was a monster of Victorian architecture, and it dominated the town skyline until softened by trees, some of which have already been planted in the foreground. Today you will find boarders from all parts of the world enjoying (let us hope) an English Public School education.

▼ Bredfield, The White House 1929 82965

Edward FitzGerald was born here in 1829. It is a stark and charmless building of the Jacobean period, rented from a local squire, and Fitz did not have happy memories of it. The family had purchased nearby Boulge Hall, but were unable to move in until the widow of the former owner, a Mrs Short, died, which she insisted on NOT doing for a further 35 years.

▲ Boulge Hall 1929 8296

The family moved in at last in 1835 when Fitz was 16 years old. It is an extravagant but elegant Queen Anne mansion, and Fitz never managed to like it either. He soon moved out. Boulge Hall is no more; it was unceremoniously torn down in the last century when it proved too expensive to maintain.

◄ **Boulge Cottage 1929**
82966
FitzGerald quickly moved to a cottage on the estate, a cottage built earlier by the long-living widow, Mrs Short, as an escape from her husband! Fitz filled it with books, and enjoyed wonderful evenings of conviviality with his friends here. The original building, on the right, was thatched.

Seager's Shop on Market Hill 1929 82963
Look at the plaque between the windows: 'E F G 1860-1873'. Edward FitzGerald lived here as little more than a rather fractious paying guest in a private home. The sound of the mournful church bells ringing nearly drove him mad, but it took thirteen years before he moved on. The great name of Seagers has only just left the Market Hill, one of the last of the 'really useful' shops to go.

Little Grange 1929 82964

Fitz purchased a small farmhouse and six acres in 1864, but it was many years before he moved in. It was 'a chateau reserved for my last retirement from the stage.' Reconstruction and improvement took a considerable time, but it needed his eviction from his Market Hill rooms before he finally took the plunge and moved into Little Grange in 1874.

Edward FitzGerald's Grave at Boulge Churchyard 1929 82968

A modest gravestone in the churchyard marks Fitz's final resting place. He died in Norfolk in 1883. He had asked not to be put in the family mausoleum, as he wanted to be able to hear the birds sing. A rose was planted over the grave, grown from a hip brought from Persia; a fitting memorial.

Melton Road 1925 78754

The Thoroughfare, Woodbridge, runs seamlessly into Melton Road. The road was built in 1835 to replace the Old Weye, a most inadequate link with Melton. Some old maps show the route to be Brick Kiln Hill, named after nearby brickworks. The line of cottages is still standing. Beyond them, in the fields where modern housing now crowds in, cattle fairs were regularly held in earlier times.

Beyond Woodbridge

We leave Woodbridge and its celebrated inhabitants and make our way via Melton along the banks of the River Deben, soon to lose its tidal aspect, to discover just a few of the delights that lie to the east and north-east. Only the village of Butley is not connected with the river, and so in this volume it represents the villages of the Sandlings, that mosaic of heathland, arable farming and man-made forest that eventually runs into the North Sea.

Woodbridge and the villages beyond are united by their long histories, ancient rural traditions and the quality of their domestic and church architecture. The Sandlings formed a vital element in Woodbridge's economic development. From the Sandlings came the prosperity brought by massive sheep farming since the Middle Ages; the arable hinterland grew food which sustained the population or which, in the case of carrots in the 18th century, town ships could carry off to the London markets; and the massive air-bases of the modern period, culminating with the American occupation of over 40 years, were sited in the Sandlings.

Wickham Market deserves our close examination. It served a rural community for generations, and at one time housed small engineering enterprises with high reputations across the east of England. The River Deben runs through the edge of the town, and we trace it back to Glevering Bridge, where our journey ends.

▲ **Melton, The Street c1965** M268024
This view is close to the heart of Melton, which itself boasts some fine early buildings.
The name of Skoulding is recorded as early as 1868, when William Skoulding sold
groceries and drapery and was the sub-postmaster. Nearby was the old Melton Gaol
which housed Protestant martyrs, burnt at Ipswich for heresy in 1558.

▼ **The Melton Grange Hotel c1965** W128067 Proudly looking towards Woodbridge from its lofty position, the hotel, built as a private mansion, boasts almost every architectural feature employed by man since the Middle Ages, including a crenellated roofline, Tudoresque chimneys, Dutch gables and a multitude of Victorian embellishments. What a shock for the townspeople when it closed for business a few years ago.

Melton, High Street c1955 M268007
The view is taken from the Horse and Groom, looking back towards Woodbridge. The cottages on the immediate right are still standing, but the next block has been demolished. The cafe on the corner is now a fish bar and restaurant, still providing sustenance for the villagers.

◀ **Melton, The Asylum 189▮**
37324
This stark Victorian institutio▮
the psychiatric hospital kno▮
as St Audreys, overlooked
Melton for two centuries,
housing hundreds of inmate▮
in vast and overcrowded
wards. Modern medicine an▮
more enlightened practices
for dealing with mental illnes▮
have wrought a huge chang▮
The buildings that remain
are now private dwellings.
Even 'The Old Mortuary'
was recently sold as a bijou
residence!

Melton, Station Road c1965 M268021
The Horse and Groom, a fine 18th-century coaching inn, stands on the corner of the road leading to the River Deben and the railway station. On the right, past the line of cottages, a white weather-boarded building, Anvil Antiques, purveyed both ancient bric-a-brac and modern ornate metal crafts. Behind the pub is the Victorian church of St Andrew, a replacement for 'the old church' which lay a mile outside Melton.

▼ **Ufford**
The Church 1894 33989
Before crossing the river at Wilford we make a short detour to the tiny village of Ufford. The beautifully proportioned church of St Mary with its flint facing is renowned for its finely-carved lacy-pinnacled font cover, the finest to be found in East Anglia. The cover almost reaches the roof, and is crowned with a pious pelican. But all is not well in Ufford. . .

◄ **Ufford**
The Stocks at St Mary's Church 1894
33990
. . . hints of past demeanours lurk outside the church in the shape of a stocks and whipping post, the latter somewhat truncated since 1894.

▲ **Melton, The Station Hotel c1955** M268006
Making our way down towards the Wilford Bridge on the way to the golf course or the villages of the Sandlings, we pass the Station Hotel, built in the late 1850s when the railway eventually arrived. Today, light engineering works crowd in on the left. Few passengers now alight at Melton station, and the hotel has become a quality food retail outlet.

◄ **Melton, Wilford Bridge 1894** 33988
The first crossing on the River Deben, the bridge was built, as the place-name suggests, at a convenient fording point on the river, but only at low tide. Small commercial vessels could certainly come as far as Wilford in the 19th century. The hill behind, just in view, is the gallows hill where local villains were hung, and publicly displayed as a warning to others.

Melton, Wilford Bridge 1898 42775

For once the photographer has arrived at low tide. Interesting comparisons can be made with the photograph of 1894, No 33988 (previous page); now it is possible to see how the river could be easily forded at the right time. Is that the new golf clubhouse on the hill? It was built between the Frith visits.

Bromeswell, Woodbridge Golf Club 1898 42777

The club was founded in 1893, and this handsome clubhouse, designed as a cricket pavilion, opened two years later. The proximity of the course to a busy rifle range led to a number of incidents and complaints, especially when the Hon Sec suffered a 'near miss'. The shooters moved their range, commenting that the only injuries on the heath to date had been those inflicted by golf balls on sheep.

Bromeswell, Fryer's Bridge over the Sutton Road 1929 82962
Old Harrovian F E R Fryer 'improved' the golf course in 1908, placing a green and a tee on the opposite side of the Melton to Sutton highway, inviting the players to drive the chasm twice. Hazards included the real threat of injury to innocent travellers below, and great inconvenience to golfers whose shots ended up on the road. This wooden bridge carried the players over the deep cutting.

Bromeswell, Woodbridge Golf Club and Fryer's Bridge 1929 82961
A golfer's eye view of the 18th green and the 19th hole. A few years after the picture was taken, the increased traffic on the road below necessitated the removal of Fryer's Bridge, such an unique feature of the course, and the golfers were forced to remain on the Bromeswell side.

▼ Bromeswell, Woodbridge Golf Club c1955 M268004

Extensions to the clubhouse commenced almost immediately after its construction, and by 1955 the building was something of an untidy sprawl. In earlier times, energetic members who cycled to the course were asked not to park their bikes under the verandas. Today a grand new brick building offers facilities which make Woodbridge Golf Club, together with its magnificent courses, one of the finest in East Anglia.

▼ Butley, The Old School c1955 B618007

This early Victorian school stands next to the church. Children were educated on this rather isolated site for over 150 years. The headmaster's smart car and the junior teacher's bicycle may be identified.

▲ Butley, The Church c1955 B618006

Six miles to the east of Woodbridge, this charming parish church of St John the Baptist has a 13th-century tower and two Norman doorways. It still retains its partially thatched roof.

◄ **Butley, The Street c1955**
B618002
This view is a striking example of the unchanging life in many Suffolk villages; the scene is virtually unchanged in half a century. Residents may not all service the agricultural hinterland these days; they are as likely to be software engineers working in Ipswich.

Butley, High Corner c1955 B618011
A picture of charming rusticity in the heart of the Sandlings, just a few miles from the sea. 'The dry heaths,' wrote Arthur Young 200 years ago, 'are to be profitably managed only by sheep being made the principle object'. The sheep have gone; tourists sustain the economy in a landscape sometimes affronted by modern agricultural methods.

▲ **Wickham Market
Market Hill 1929**
82046

◄ **Wickham Market
The Market Hill 1929**
82048

Wickham Market, as
its name suggests, has
a long trading history.
The small bustling
town is centred around
this square, filled with
shops and services and
buildings of a fine range
of architectural styles. A
handsome town pump
dominates the centre
of the square which in
1929 was open and
rather stark . . .
although the motor car
had certainly arrived!
(see 82046, above)

Wickham Market, Pettistree Church 1929 82060
Pettistree adjoins the main road into Wickham Market. The 15th-century church of St Peter and St Paul has a fine square tower and distinctive flint flushwork. The impressive timber-framed Greyhound Inn stands against the south side of the churchyard. Inn and church now form, with the green, the centre of the modern village.

Wickham Market, The Market Hill c1960 W94040
The Market Hill was softened in appearance in the 1960s by skilful tree-planting, and the increase in traffic had led to the provision of a car-park. The fine and unusual spire and octagonal tower of All-Saints Church oversees the landscape, as it does today.

Wickham Market, The White Hart Hotel c1955 W94021
The Georgian White Hart Hotel with its distinctive porch once dominated the Market Hill, and indeed perhaps the social life of the town. The old coaching inn has now ceased trading, and the building is divided into a series of shops, offices and private residences. Also sadly lost is W Taylor and Son, in the timbered building; people drove across from Woodbridge to shop there! The usage of these shops has changed, but the liveliness and diversity of the Market Hill remains.

**Wickham Market
Middle Hill 1929**

82051

A car struggles up the hill towards the market square, embracing most of the road in his determination to get there. Today Middle Hill boasts a pavement on both sides, testament to the increase in traffic. This was once the main Ipswich to Lowestoft road, crowded with heavy lorries. A few cottages have been modernised, but the street is remarkably unchanged.

Wickham Market, Rackham's Mill c1960 W94041
This picturesque range of buildings stands on the river at the eastern edge of the town. A dynasty of Rackhams has operated the water mill and steam roller-mill, and today it provides animal feeds, pet foods and other goods. The complex is in an excellent state of preservation, and it is much visited by molinologists. The river runs towards us on the right and the tail race of the waterwheel joins from the left.

Wickham Market, Glevering Bridge 1929 82055
The road winds its way out of Wickham Market, over Glevering Bridge towards Easton and Framlingham, passing a delightful little golf course just through the trees on the left, out to the delights of the Suffolk countryside and the realms of another tome.

Index

FRITH PRODUCTS & SERVICES

Francis Frith would doubtless be pleased to know that the pioneering publishing venture he started in 1860 still continues today. Over a hundred and forty years later, The Francis Frith Collection continues in the same innovative tradition and is now one of the foremost publishers of vintage photographs in the world. Some of the current activities include:

INTERIOR DECORATION

Today Frith's photographs can be seen framed and as giant wall murals in thousands of pubs, restaurants, hotels, banks, retail stores and other public buildings throughout the country. In every case they enhance the unique local atmosphere of the places they depict and provide reminders of gentler days in an increasingly busy and frenetic world.

PRODUCT PROMOTIONS

Frith products are used by many major companies to promote the sales of their own products or to reinforce their own history and heritage. Frith promotions have been used by Hovis bread, Courage beers, Scots Porage Oats, Colman's mustard, Cadbury's foods, Mellow Birds coffee, Dunhill pipe tobacco, Guinness, and Bulmer's Cider.

GENEALOGY AND FAMILY HISTORY

As the interest in family history and roots grows world-wide, more and more people are turning to Frith's photographs of Great Britain for images of the towns, villages and streets where their ancestors lived; and, of course, photographs of the churches and chapels where their ancestors were christened, married and buried are an essential part of every genealogy tree and family album.

FRITH PRODUCTS

All Frith photographs are available Framed or just as Mounted Prints and unmounted versions. These may be ordered from the address below. Other products available are - Calendars, Jigsaws, Canvas Prints, Mugs, Tea Towels, Tableware and local and prestige books.

THE INTERNET

Over several hundred thousand Frith photographs can be viewed and purchased on the internet through the Frith websites!

For more detailed information on Frith products, look at **www.francisfrith.com**

See the complete list of Frith Books at: www.francisfrith.com
This web site is regularly updated with the latest list of publications from The Francis Frith Collection. If you wish to buy books relating to another part of the country that your local bookshop does not stock, you may purchase on-line.

For further information, trade, or author enquiries please contact us at the address below:
The Francis Frith Collection, Unit 19 Kingsmead Business Park, Gillingham, Dorset SP8 5FB.
Tel: +44 (0)1722 716 376   Email: sales@francisfrith.co.uk

See Frith products on the internet at www.francisfrith.com

FREE PRINT OF YOUR CHOICE
CHOOSE A PHOTOGRAPH FROM THIS BOOK

+ POSTAGE

Mounted Print
Overall size 14 x 11 inches (355 x 280mm)

TO RECEIVE YOUR FREE PRINT

Choose any Frith photograph in this book

Simply complete the Voucher opposite and return it with your payment (to cover postage and handling) and we will print the photograph of your choice in SEPIA (size 11 x 8 inches) and supply it in a cream mount ready to frame (overall size 14 x 11 inches).

Order additional Mounted Prints
at HALF PRICE - £19.00 each (normally £38.00)

If you would like to order more Frith prints from this book, possibly as gifts for friends and family, you can buy them at half price (with no additional postage costs).

Have your Mounted Prints framed

For an extra £20.00 per print you can have your mounted print(s) framed in an elegant polished wood and gilt moulding, overall size 16 x 13 inches (no additional postage required).

IMPORTANT!

❶ Please note: aerial photographs and photographs with a reference number starting with a "Z" are not Frith photographs and cannot be supplied under this offer.

❷ Offer valid for delivery to one UK address only.

❸ These special prices are only available if you use this form to order. You must use the ORIGINAL VOUCHER on this page (no copies permitted). We can only despatch to one UK address.

❹ This offer cannot be combined with any other offer.

As a customer your name & address will be stored by Frith but not sold or rented to third parties. Your data will be used for the purpose of this promotion only.

Send completed Voucher form to:

The Francis Frith Collection,
19 Kingsmead Business Park, Gillingham,
Dorset SP8 5FB

Voucher for *FREE* and Reduced Price *Frith Prints*

Please do not photocopy this voucher. Only the original is valid, so please fill it in, cut it out and return it to us with your order.

Picture ref no	Page no	Qty	Mounted @ £19.00	Framed + £20.00	Total Cost £
		1	Free of charge*	£	£
			£19.00	£	£
			£19.00	£	£
			£19.00	£	£
			£19.00	£	£
			£19.00	£	£
Please allow 28 days for delivery. Offer available to one UK address only			* Post & handling		£3.80
			Total Order Cost		£

Title of this book . . . .

I enclose a cheque/postal order for £ . . . .
made payable to 'The Francis Frith Collection'

OR please debit my Mastercard / Visa / Maestro card, details below

Card Number:

Issue No (Maestro only):   Valid from (Maestro):

Card Security Number: Expires:

Signature:

Name Mr/Mrs/Ms . . . .

Address . . . .

. . . .

. . . .

. . . . Postcode . . . .

Daytime Tel No . . . .

Email . . . .

Valid to 31/12/24

Free Print – see overleaf

Can you help us with information about any of the Frith photographs in this book?

We are gradually compiling an historical record for each of the photographs in the Frith archive. It is always fascinating to find out the names of the people shown in the pictures, as well as insights into the shops, buildings and other features depicted.

If you recognize anyone in the photographs in this book, or if you have information not already included in the author's caption, do let us know. We would love to hear from you, and will try to publish it in future books or articles.

An Invitation from The Francis Frith Collection to Share Your Memories

The 'Share Your Memories' feature of our website allows members of the public to add personal memories relating to the places featured in our photographs, or comment on others already added. Seeing a place from your past can rekindle forgotten or long held memories. Why not visit the website, find photographs of places you know well and add YOUR story for others to read and enjoy? We would love to hear from you!

www.francisfrith.com/memories

Our production team

Frith books are produced by a small dedicated team at offices near Salisbury. Most have worked with the Frith Collection for many years. All have in common one quality: they have a passion for the Frith Collection.

Frith Books and Gifts

We have a wide range of books and gifts available on our website utilising our photographic archive, many of which can be individually personalised.

www.francisfrith.com